READY, SET, GAME!

ONLINE GAMING

BY BETSY RATHBURN

TORQUE™

BELLWETHER MEDIA • MINNEAPOLIS, MN

TORQUE brims with excitement perfect for thrill-seekers of all kinds. Discover daring survival skills, explore uncharted worlds, and marvel at mighty engines and extreme sports. In *Torque* books, anything can happen. Are you ready?

This edition first published in 2021 by Bellwether Media, Inc.

Library of Congress Cataloging-in-Publication Data

Names: Rathburn, Betsy, author.
Title: Online gaming / by Betsy Rathburn.
Description: Minneapolis, MN : Bellwether Media, Inc., [2021] | Series: Torque: ready, set, game! | Includes bibliographical references and index. | Audience: Ages 7-12 | Audience: Grades 4-6 | Summary: "Amazing photography accompanies engaging information about online gaming. The combination of high-interest subject matter and light text is intended for students in grades 3 through 7"– Provided by publisher.
Identifiers: LCCN 2020048061 (print) | LCCN 2020048062 (ebook) | ISBN 9781644874585 (library binding) | ISBN 9781648342516 (paperback) | ISBN 9781648341359 (ebook)
Subjects: LCSH: Internet games–Juvenile literature. | Internet games–History–Juvenile literature. | Internet games industry–Juvenile literature.
Classification: LCC GV1469.15 .R39 2021 (print) | LCC GV1469.15 (ebook) | DDC 794.8-dc23
LC record available at https://lccn.loc.gov/2020048061
LC ebook record available at https://lccn.loc.gov/2020048062

Editor: Elizabeth Neuenfeldt   Designer: Brittany McIntosh

Printed in the United States of America, North Mankato, MN.

TABLE OF CONTENTS

BATTLE READY

Time to drop! Your team jumps out of the Battle Bus. You aim for an empty place on the map. Will it be overrun with enemies?

After you land, the safe zone starts shrinking. You run to the circle and find a supply crate. Now you have what you need to win the match in *Fortnite*!

FRED INSTEAD

The Loot Llama drops special items in *Fortnite*. The character even has a name. It is called Fred!

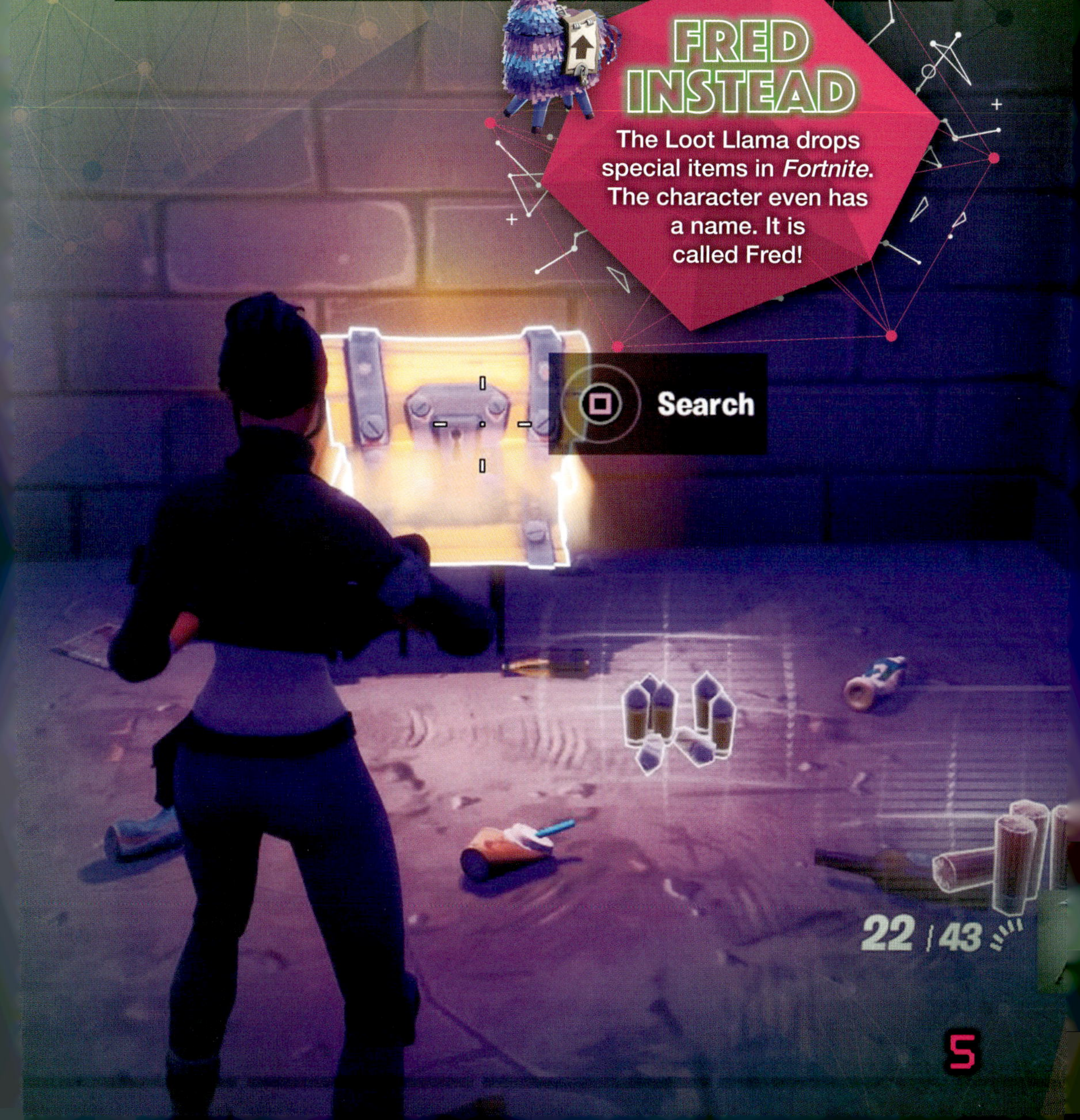

ONLINE GAMING HISTORY

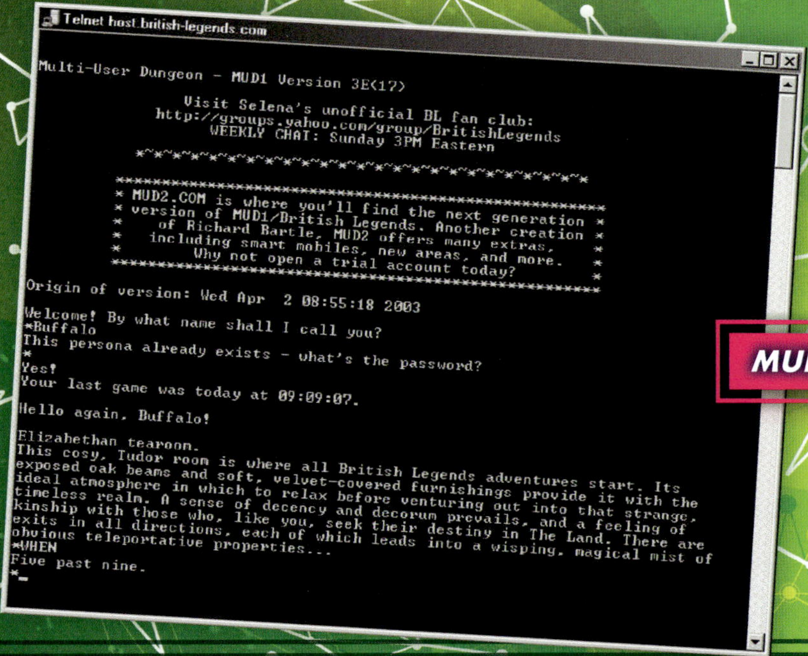

MUD1

Online gaming began in the 1970s. Computer **networks** let people play together. Many colleges had computer networks. They were not connected with computers outside of the school.

One of the first games to be played on a network was called *MUD1*. This text-based game was created in England at the University of Essex in 1978.

ONLINE GAMING TIMELINE

1978
MUD1 is created at the University of Essex

1980
The University of Essex is added to the ARPANET, bringing more players to *MUD1*

1984
Island of Kesmai is made

1988
Nintendo releases the Family Computer Network System, an early online gaming service in Japan

1990
Sega introduces the Sega Meganet

1999
Sega releases *ChuChu Rocket!*, the first popular online console game

XBOX LIVE

2002
Xbox Live is launched

2006
PlayStation Network begins

PlayStation Network

NINTENDO NETWORK

2012
Nintendo Network is launched

By 1980, the **ARPANET** brought *MUD1* to more players. This computer network was an early form of the internet. Many more computer games followed!

In 1988, Nintendo brought online gaming to consoles in Japan. Sega followed in 1990 with Sega Meganet for the Sega Genesis. But it was expensive. **Graphics** also took a long time to load. Few people could play.

Flicky

MEGANET GAMES

Many Sega Meganet games could not be played on consoles offline. But *Fatal Labyrinth* and *Flicky* were later made available to offline players!

ONLINE GAMING THROUGH TIME

1978

MUD1

1984

Island of Kesmai

1988

Air Warrior

1990

Tel-Tel Stadium

1999

ChuChu Rocket!

1999

EverQuest

2001

RuneScape

2004

World of Warcraft

ChuChu Rocket!

The 1990s brought better internet. New **modems** let people download games more quickly. Sega's Dreamcast was the first console with a built-in modem. People loved its 1999 game *ChuChu Rocket!* It was the first popular online game for consoles.

Xbox Live launched in 2002. Soon, gamers could go online to play *NBA 2K2, Midtown Madness,* and many other games!

NBA 2K2

OTHER OPTIONS

PlayStation Network launched in 2006. In 2012, the Nintendo Network began. Like Xbox Live, these services continue to let people play their favorite games online today!

ONLINE GAMING TODAY

Today, online gaming is more popular than ever. High-speed internet means games can be more complicated. It also helps people connect more quickly on computers, consoles, and smartphones. Gamers can even play together across different devices!

Other technology lets gamers communicate easily. **Headsets** with microphones let players talk to people around the world!

There are many types of online games. Players can explore worlds in **MMORPGs**. Other games have more **competition**. The 2017 game *Splatoon 2* and 2018's *Super Smash Bros. Ultimate* let players battle against friends online.

MMORPG MVP

The most popular MMORPG is *World of Warcraft*. This 2004 game has about 5 million players!

Splatoon 2

Battle royales also make competition fun. *Fortnite* and *Fall Guys* are especially popular. *Fortnite* has over 350 million players!

Fall Guys

GAME SPOTLIGHT

GAME *Among Us*

YEAR 2018

TYPE multiplayer

DESCRIPTION Players are divided into Crewmates and Impostors, and then let loose into a space-themed world. They must work together to complete tasks and figure out each player's role.

Not all online games are competitive. *Minecraft* lets players craft online with friends. In the 2020 game *Animal Crossing: New Horizons*, players connect online to trade items or go fishing!

POPULAR ONLINE GAMES

(BY NUMBER OF GAMES SOLD AND DOWNLOADED)

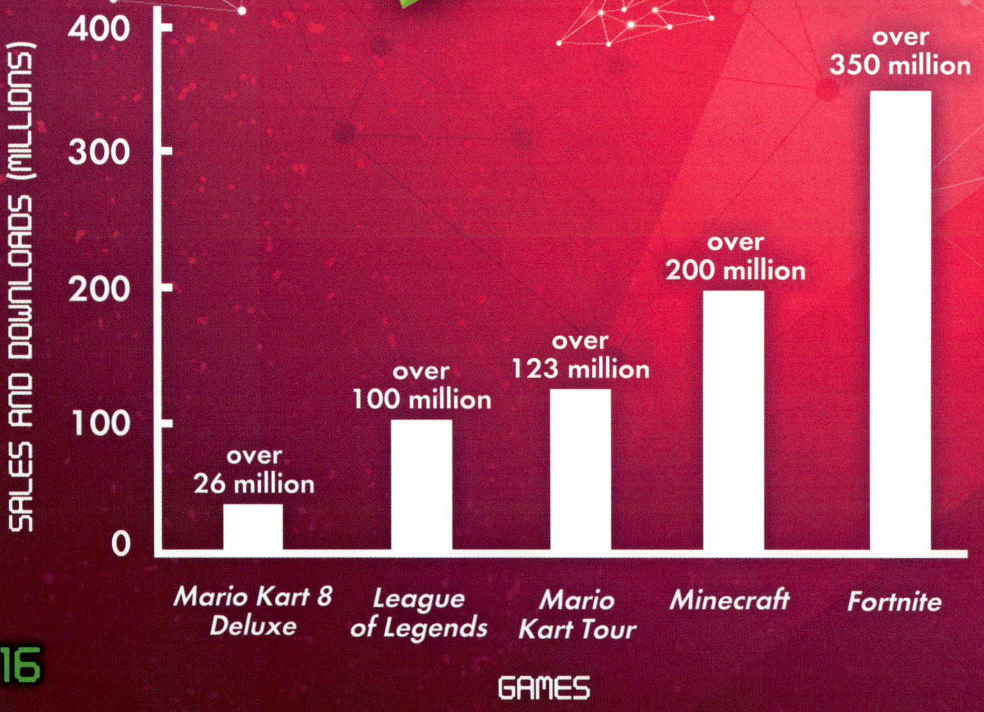

In other games, online players can team up to beat the clock. The game *Overcooked! 2* lets players battle **obstacles** as they race to serve meals.

THE ONLINE GAMING COMMUNITY

Fortnite World Cup

Many people form communities in online games. Some games have groups called **guilds**. Players join to make friends and play together.

Some online games have competitions. **Esports** events draw many viewers. In 2019, the first *Fortnite* World Cup was held. Over 2.3 million people viewed the event on YouTube and Twitch!

ONLINE GAMING EVENT SPOTLIGHT

EVENT *Fortnite* World Cup

GAME *Fortnite*

PURPOSE find the best *Fortnite* players in the world

WHEN IT HAPPENS once each year

WHERE IT HAPPENS United States

RECENT WINNER Bugha (2019)

Online gaming is even used to help people. In 2020, Gamers Without Borders hosted a **charity** *Fortnite* event. Teams competed to give winnings to help organizations fighting against **COVID-19**. They donated $2 million!

New online games come out every year. Online gamers will continue to have fun, compete, and help others!

Animal Crossing: New Horizons

GLOSSARY

ARPANET—Advanced Research Projects Agency Network; ARPANET was an early form of the internet.

battle royales—games in which many players compete to be the last player standing

charity—related to an organization or event that gives money to those in need

competition—an event in which more than one person is trying to win the same thing

COVID-19—a virus that can affect the ability to breathe; COVID-19 spread around the world to affect millions of people in 2020.

esports—multiplayer video games that are played competitively for spectators

graphics—images displayed on a computer screen

guilds—groups that players can join in certain games

headsets—devices worn on the head that let players hear and speak to others

MMORPGs—massively multiplayer online role-playing games; MMORPGs let players create and move around an online world and interact with other players.

modems—devices that let computers connect to the internet

networks—systems that connect many computers

obstacles—things that block movement or progress

TO LEARN MORE

AT THE LIBRARY

Gregory, Josh. *How Fortnite Was Made.* Ann Arbor, Mich.: Cherry Lake Publishing, 2020.

Rathburn, Betsy. *Computer Gaming.* Minneapolis, Minn.: Bellwether Media, 2021.

Sherman, Jill, and Alexis Roumanis. *Online Games.* New York, N.Y.: AV2 by Weigl, 2019.

ON THE WEB

FACTSURFER

Factsurfer.com gives you a safe, fun way to find more information.

1. Go to www.factsurfer.com.

2. Enter "online gaming" into the search box and click 🔍.

3. Select your book cover to see a list of related content.

INDEX

The images in this book are reproduced through the courtesy of: Photoongraphy, front cover (left); robtek, front cover (middle); Memory Photographic, front cover (right); *Fortnite*/ Bellwether Media, pp. 4, 5 (bottom); Epic Games, p. 5 (top); *MUD1*, p. 6; Microsoft/ Wikipedia, p. 7 (Xbox Live); Nintendo/ Wikipedia, p. 7 (Nintendo Network); Sony/ Wikipedia, p. 7 (PlayStation Network); ArcadeImages/ Alamy, p. 8; *MUD1*/ DeMatt, p. 9 (*MUD1*); *Island of Kesmai*/ Kesmai, p. 9 (*Island of Kesmai*); *Air Warrior*/ Randy Green, p. 9 (*Air Warrior*); *Tel-Tel Stadium*/ Sunsoft, p. 9 (*Tel-Tel Stadium*); *ChuChu Rocket!*/ Lewis Cox, p. 9 (*ChuChu Rocket!*); *EverQuest*/ SuperBitsAndBob, p. 9 (*EverQuest*); *RuneScape*/ mr extremez, p. 9 (*RuneScape*); *World of Warcraft*/ Blizzard, p. 9 (*World of Warcraft*); *ChuChu Rocket!*, p. 10; *NBA 2K*/ 2K Games, p. 11; JJFraq, p. 12; Gorodenkoff, p. 13; Casimiro PT, p. 14 (top); *Splatoon 2*/ Nintendo, p. 14 (bottom); *Fall Guys: Ultimate Knockout*/ Mediatonic, p. 15 (top); *Among Us*/ InnerSloth, p. 15 (bottom); *Overcooked! 2*/ Team17, p. 17; dpa picture alliance/ Alamy, pp. 18-19; Leonard Zhukovsky, p. 20.